UNDERSEA SCHOOL

Disney · PIXAR

FINDING NEMO

# Undersea Explorer

by Adrienne Mason

Scholastic Inc.

New York · Toronto · London · Auckland · Sydney
Mexico City · New Delhi · Hong Kong · Buenos Aires

Designer: Julia Sarno
Interior illustrations by Yancey Labat

Photo Credits:
Page 12: (school of fish) CORBIS.
Page 20: (dolphin, manatee) Doug Perrine/SeaPics.com; (sea lions) © Photodisc Blue (RF)/Getty Images;
(sea otter) James D. Watt/SeaPics.com.
Page 21: (great white shark) Marty Snyderman/Visuals Unlimited; (manta ray) © Ian Cartwright/Photodisc Blue/Getty Images.
Page 22: (clown fish) © Georgette Douwma/Photodisc Green (RF)/Getty Images; (sea horse) Bill Kamin/Visuals Unlimited;
(butterfly fish) Ken Lucas/Visuals Unlimited; (blue tang) © Royalty-Free/Corbis; (sea turtle) Doug Perrine/SeaPics.com.
Page 23: (octopus) © James Gritz/Photodisc Blue/Getty Images; (sea star) Gerald & Buff Corsi/Visuals Unlimited.
Page 24: (oyster) © Hal Beral/Corbis; (lobster) © Ian Cartwright/Photodisc Blue/Getty Images; (giant clam) © Ian Cartwright/Photodisc Green
(RF)/Getty Images; (sea wasp jellyfish) Gary Bell/SeaPics.com; (sea snail) © Brandon Cole/Corbis.
Page 25: (copepod) © Douglas Wilson/Corbis.
Page 27: (tube worm) © Royalty-Free/Corbis; (thorny oyster) © Hal Beral/Corbis.
Page 28: (baleen) Michael S. Nolan/SeaPics.com.
Page 29: (squid) © Mike Kelly/Image Bank/Getty Images; (sea star) Dr. James P. McVey/NOAA Sea Grant Program.
Page 30-32: (background) Jeff Hunter/Photographer's Choice/Getty Images.
Page 30: (harbor seal) © Photodisc Blue (RF)/Getty Images; (common dolphin) Jeff Pantukhuff/SeaPics.com;
(sperm whale) © Amos Nachoum/Corbis; (great white shark) Marty Snyderman/Visuals Unlimited.
Page 31: (brain coral) © Comstock Images (RF)/Getty Images; (plate coral) © Ian Cartwright/Photodisc Green (RF)/Getty Images;
(staghorn coral) © Royalty-Free/Corbis; (star coral) © James Gritz/Photodisc Blue/Getty Images.
Page 32: (tuna) © Amos Nachoum/Corbis; (swordfish) Eleonara de Sabata/SeaPics.com; (jellyfish) © Rubberball Productions/Getty Images.
Page 33: (sand dollar) © Jeffrey Rotman/Corbis; (moon snail) © Jeffrey Rotman/Corbis; (background) © Jack Hollingsworth/Photodisc Green
(RF)/Getty Images.
Page 34: (tidal pool with starfish) © Art Wolfe/Image Bank/Getty Images; (barnacles) © Douglas Wilson/Corbis; (mussels) © Alex Fradkin/
Photodisc Blue/Getty Images; (background) Doug Perrine/SeaPics.com.
Page 36: (common murres) © National Geographic ; (hagfish) © Brandon Cole/Corbis.
Page 37: (coral reef background) © Ian Cartwright/Photodisc Blue/Getty Images.

Published by Scholastic Inc., 557 Broadway, New York, NY 10012, by arrangement
with Disney Licensed Publishing. SCHOLASTIC, UNDERSEA SCHOOL, and
associated logos are trademarks and/or registered trademarks of Scholastic Inc.

ISBN 0-439-78361-5

12 11 10 9 8 7 6 5 4 3 2 1     5 6 7 8 9 10/0

Printed in the U.S.A.
First Scholastic printing, May 2005

# Table of Contents

# Welcome to UNDERSEA SCHOOL

**Nemo**
*clown fish*

**H**I, there! I'm Nemo. Did you know we have a lot in common? We both have friends, a home, and a school. It's just that I'm a clown fish, and you're a human. And while you probably have a home on land, go to school in a building, and play with your human friends—I live on a coral reef, go to school under the sea, and have friends who are fish!

We also have one more thing in common—we're both students who like to *dive* into learning! We can discover lots of amazing things about the ocean. Did you know that the ocean is home to:

- **sharks with 20 rows of teeth.**

- **fish as prickly as porcupines.**

- **animals tinier than a grain of sand.**

- **and whales bigger than buses!**

> Whale?
> I speak whale. Oh, hi,
> I'm Dory. Did I tell
> you I speak whale?

There are lots of other cool creatures that live in the ocean, too. Do you want to go to Undersea School with me? In our first adventure, we'll find out . . .

**DORY**
*blue tang*

- **why the ocean is salty.**

- **what whales and sea stars eat.**

- **how coral reefs are made of living creatures.**

- **and so much more!**

You can meet all my friends, too. Can you swim? Don't worry if you can't. Just grab my lucky fin and dive right in!

# Chapter 1: The Wonders of Water

## Let's start our adventure with a question. How many oceans are there in the world?

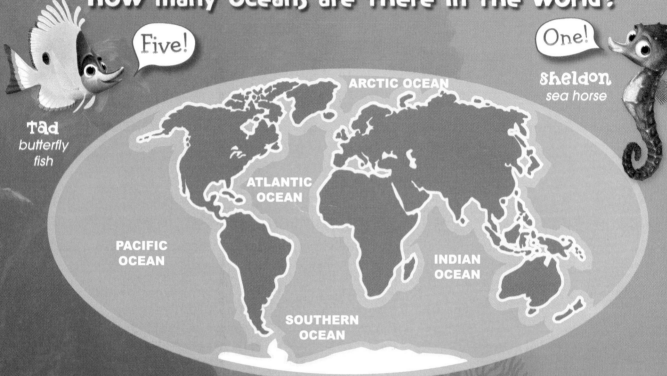

**Five!** — Tad, butterfly fish

**One!** — Sheldon, sea horse

ARCTIC OCEAN

ATLANTIC OCEAN

PACIFIC OCEAN

INDIAN OCEAN

SOUTHERN OCEAN

Tad, Sheldon—you're both right! If you look on this map, you can see that a lot of the Earth is covered by ocean. In fact, it might make more sense if our planet was named Ocean instead of Earth! On a map, the ocean is divided into five different oceans—the *Pacific*, *Atlantic*, *Indian*, *Arctic*, and *Southern* (also called the *Antarctic*). These oceans are all connected, so it's like Earth has one ocean. Trace your finger along the map, from one ocean to the next, and you'll see how the world is connected by one huge, salty swimming pool.

## pass the salt

Did you ever wonder why the ocean tastes so salty? Water in rivers and streams flows over the land and picks up the salts that are naturally found in soil and rocks. Rivers and streams carry this salt into the ocean. This has happened again and again for millions of years. So, the ocean has become one salty place!

# Apple Pie Ocean

If the Earth was an apple pie cut into four equal pieces, only one piece would be land. The other three pieces would be water, and almost all of that water would be found in the ocean. Only a small amount of Earth's water is found in lakes and rivers.

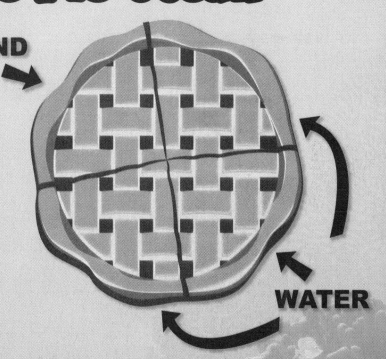

**LAND**

**WATER**

**Marlin**
*clown fish*

Hey, there! I'm Nemo's dad, Marlin. Do you know why fish are so smart? Because they swim in schools! Ha! Get it?

## water, water, everywhere

There's lots of water in this great ocean of ours, but there's water in other places, too. Water is everywhere around you on Earth. Sure, it's easy to see all of this water when you're in the middle of the ocean. But you can see water on land, too—in lakes, rivers, puddles, and bathtubs. But water isn't always easy to see. Sometimes it's hidden.

Where is all of this hidden water? Why, some of it is inside you!

Some fish swim in large groups, called schools, for safety.

In fact, there's water inside every plant and animal in the ocean and on land. Do you know how much you weigh? Well, more than half of your weight is water. Water makes up most of your brain, your blood, and your bones. Humans need to drink plenty of water every day. All living things need water— whether they live in the ocean or on land.

See? We're a lot alike. We both need water to live!

## CLOWNING AROUND!

**Q:** Why do fish swim in salt water?

**A:** Because pepper water makes them sneeze!

# That's a Mouthful, Mate!

G'day, mate! The name's Bruce. If you come across any BIG words while you're in Undersea School, no worries. My friends, Chum and Anchor, and I will help you take a bite out of them by explaining what they mean. Let's get a head start with this word: *evaporation* (you'll find it on the next page). When something evaporates, it changes from a liquid to a gas. Puddles evaporate as the sun warms up the water.

**BRUCE**
*great white shark*

13

# Water's Wild Ride

Have you ever been on a water slide? If you could hitch a ride on a drop of water, you'd be in for a wild ride, too. You'd travel from the ocean to the clouds and back! The world's water is always on the move. Here's what happens:

1. As the sun warms water on Earth, some of the water changes into gas and rises into the air. This is called *evaporation*.

2. This gas collects in the air and forms clouds. When the clouds meet cooler air, the water changes from a gas to a liquid—like rain.

3. Finally, the rain falls back to Earth and the cycle starts all over again.

So, this water I'm swimming through could have once been in a cloud.

Or frozen in an iceberg!

**pearl**
*octopus*

## water Forever

Did you know that the water we're swimming in might have once rained down on a dinosaur? That's right! Every drop of Earth's water has been here forever.

# Eat, Drink, and Breathe Water!

Water comes in three forms: solid, liquid, and gas. In the glass below, the solid water (ice) is in the liquid water. When water is in the form of gas, it is called water vapor. Water vapor is invisible, so you can't see it in a glass of water. But you can be sure that it's in the air all around you!

Hey, water is even older than my dad!

**squirt**
*sea turtle*

15

# Chapter 2: The Ocean in Motion

Getting a little tired from all this swimming? Let's put up our fins and relax! Even if we stop flapping our fins, though, we'd still keep moving slowly. That's because the ocean is always moving. Here's Crush to show you how waves and currents keep the ocean in motion.

**Crush**
*sea turtle*

## catch a wave

Hey, little dude! The wonderful motion of the ocean is caused when wind blows across water and creates *waves*. That's all it takes. Try it for yourself: You can make your own waves when you blow on a bowl of soup. Waves come in different sizes. Gentle winds make small waves. Strong winds that blow over long distances create big waves.

> Big wind for big waves! Sweet!

But you know, little dude, waves have to stop eventually. So, they stop at the beach. A righteous place to stop, if you ask me! When the bottom of the wave hits the seafloor, the bottom stops moving, but the top keeps on going. The wave kind of breaks in half. That's why crashing waves are sometimes called breakers. Cowabunga!

## Tidal Tales

If you were at the beach, you might notice that the ocean water moves up high onto the sand for part of the day. This is called high tide. *Tides* are the daily rise and fall of the world's oceans. They are caused when the moon acts like a big magnet and "pulls" on the Earth's water. Water rises up in a bulge on the side of the Earth that faces the moon.

## CLOWNING AROUND!

**Q:** I said hello to the ocean today. What do you think it said back?

**A:** Nothing. It just waved!

# cruising on currents

Grab shell, dude! We're on the East Australian Current—also known as the E.A.C. Just like there are rivers that carry water across land, there are **currents** that carry awesome amounts of water through the oceans. Currents help mix warm and cold water. They also move food around the world's oceans.

Animals can ride on ocean currents, too. Sometimes they have totally weird traveling partners. Stuff like running shoes, hockey equipment, and toys have fallen off cargo and cruise ships. These lost objects then start a long trip on ocean currents.

## Something's Fishy

A few months after a container of expensive running shoes fell off a ship far out at sea, currents started to deliver the shoes to beaches. It was hard to find a matching pair, but smart shoe searchers found a way to solve this problem. They held "swap meets" with other shoe searchers to help single shoes find their match!

**Gill**
*moorish idol*

Bzzzzzzzzzzz! Whoa, dude, that sounds like the recess bell. Let's take a break and play a game!

# FISHY FUN: A Recess Riddle

Hooray! It's recess! My friends and I are getting ready to play our favorite game. To find out what it is, complete the sentences below by filling in the blanks. If you need help, turn back to pages 10–17. After you have all your answers, write the letters that have a number under them in the correct boxes at the bottom of the page—and you'll find out what game we're about to play! (*Check your answers on page 38.*)

**1.** Most of Earth's water is in the  O C <u>E</u> A <u>N</u> .
                                          9        6

**2.** The five oceans are named: Pacific, Arctic, Southern, Indian, and
<u>A</u> T L <u>A</u> N T I C.
 1       10

**3.** Water can be a solid, gas, or  L <u>I</u> Q <u>U</u> I D.
                                      2      3

**4.** The  W <u>I</u> N <u>D</u>  makes waves in the ocean.
                  7

**5.** The salt in the ocean comes from soil and  <u>R</u> O C K <u>S</u>.
                                                               11

**6.** Waves stop at the  B <u>E</u> A C H.
                              5

**7.** E.A.C. stands for East Australian  C U R <u>R</u> E N T.
                                                4

**8.** Some fish swim in large groups, called  S C H O O <u>L</u> S, for safety.
                                                           8

| T | I | D | E |   | A | N | D |   | S | E | A - K |
|---|---|---|---|---|---|---|---|---|---|---|---|
| 1 | 2 | 3 | 4 | 5 | 6 | 7 | 8 | 9 | 10 | 11 |

18

# Chapter 3: Who Lives in the Ocean?

Did you know there's more than just fish in the sea? There are whales, snails, scallops, seals, oysters, octopuses, and a whole lot more.

## Meet the Mammals

Whales, seals, sea otters, dolphins, and manatees are types of *marine mammals*. You're a mammal, too! Marine mammals breathe air with their lungs, so they must come to the water's surface to get their next gulp of air. All marine mammals give birth to live babies, which means they don't lay eggs like most fish, birds, and reptiles do.

Have you noticed how sleek and smooth a dolphin looks? Marine mammals, like dolphins, have bodies that are made for super-fast swimming! With their *streamlined* bodies, they can move through water very easily.

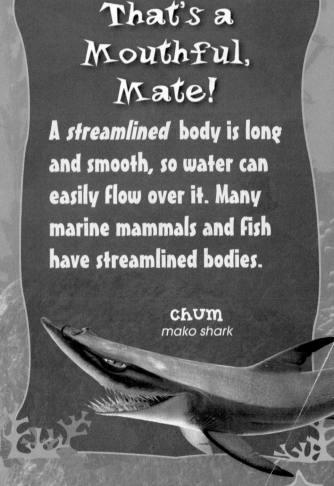

### That's a Mouthful, Mate!

A *streamlined* body is long and smooth, so water can easily flow over it. Many marine mammals and fish have streamlined bodies.

chum
*mako shark*

### CLOWNING AROUND!

**Q:** What did the dolphin say when the other dolphin stepped on his fin?

**A:** Hey! You did that on *porpoise*!

19

**Whales**, **dolphins**, and **porpoises** are marine mammals that live their entire lives in the ocean. These animals even have their babies at sea.

dolphin

Whales are not only the largest animals in the ocean, they're the largest animals in the world! The blue whale is the record holder—it's longer than three school buses!

blue whale

**Seals**, **sea lions**, and **walruses** are marine mammals that rest and give birth on land, but feed in the ocean.

sea lions

**Sea otters** are the smallest marine mammals. They eat, sleep, and give birth in the ocean.

sea otter

**Manatees** and **dugongs** (or **sea cows**) are slow-moving marine mammals that spend their entire lives in shallow, warm water.

manatee

Let's swim to the next page and meet some of my fishy friends!

# meet the fish

Smell something fishy? You should! Sharks, manta rays, sea horses, and clown fish are all types of *fish*. Unlike mammals, fish don't have lungs. Instead, they use special organs called gills to get oxygen out of the water. Most fish lay eggs to have babies.

There are thousands of kinds of fish in all shapes and sizes. Some are skinny and long like snakes, while others are larger than cars! Did you know that there are more kinds of fish in the world than all of the mammals and birds combined? That's a lot of fish to make friends with!

great white shark

**Great white sharks**, like Bruce, are among the 350 different kinds of sharks that live in the ocean. Most sharks chow down on fish or larger prey. But there are some sharks that don't eat fish and agree with Bruce's slogan: "Fish are friends...not food!"

**Manta rays,** like Mr. Ray, are very intelligent and curious creatures. Mantas eat small fish, shrimp, and plankton (see page 25) that they suck into their mouths. They can grow to be 29 feet long, and can weigh 3,000 pounds!

manta ray

**Clown fish**, like me and my dad, live inside sea anemones (uh-NEH-moe-nee) because the anemone's tentacles can sting anything that might hurt them. Clown fish don't get hurt because they brush up against the anemone every day and get used to its sting.

clown fish

**Sea horses**, like Sheldon, swim up and down rather than wiggle from side to side, like most fish. They have a curly tail that can grip onto seaweed. And male sea horses give birth to babies!

sea horse

**Blue tangs**, like Dory, are yellow as babies and turn blue as they grow up. Blue tangs have a spine at the base of their tails that they use to protect themselves.

blue tang

**Butterfly fish**, like Tad, flit about their coral reef home like butterflies. They use their long snouts to poke in-between rocks for food.

butterfly fish

## Meet the Turtles

**Sea turtles**, like Crush and Squirt, are neither mammals nor fish—they're **reptiles**. They live most of their lives in the ocean, but they come ashore to lay their eggs.

The eggs hatch and tiny turtles scurry down the beach and into the ocean. Like mammals, sea turtles have lungs, so they must come to the water's surface to breathe.

sea turtle

22

# Meet the "Spineless wonders"

Being called "spineless" is no insult in the ocean. The sea is full of spineless wonders. Animals without a spine, or backbone, are called *invertebrates*. This group of animals includes octopuses, sea stars, urchins, coral, jellyfish, snails, oysters, worms, and hundreds of other animals.

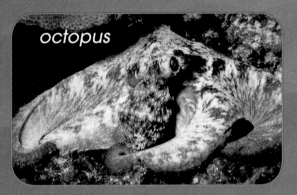
octopus

Octopuses, like Pearl, are one of the largest invertebrates. They have only one hard part—a small "beak" that they use to crunch food. The rest of their bodies are soft. To protect themselves, octopuses spurt black ink.

## That's a Mouthful, Mate!

**Invertebrate** means without a backbone, or spine. Your spine is part of your skeleton.

Anchor
hammerhead
shark

Some people call me a starfish. The only problem is, I'm not a fish. I'm an invertebrate, and really quite a star, don't you think?

Peach
sea star

Sea stars, like Peach, move about or attach themselves to surfaces using hundreds of tiny feet. They usually have five arms that form the shape of a star. If a sea star loses one of its arms, it will usually grow back within a year!

sea star

23

Oysters and clams have two shells that protect their soft bodies. To feed, they take water into their shells and strain tiny food out of the water.

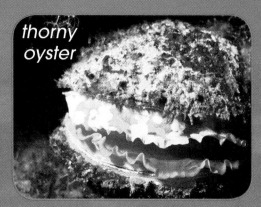
thorny oyster

lobster

Crabs and lobsters have a hard outer covering. They use their strong claws to grasp food.

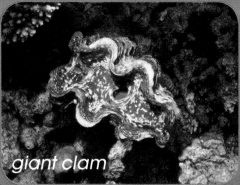
giant clam

Jellyfish are see-through, jelly-like invertebrates that float through the water. Their long tentacles are loaded with stingers that they use to capture food and protect themselves.

Snails have soft bodies that are protected by coiled shells. They move along slowly, snacking on plants and other small food as they go.

sea snail

24

jellyfish

## CLOWNING AROUND!

**Q:** What do you say to a snail that's eating all of the snacks?

**A:** Don't be *shellfish*!

# Chapter 4: What's for Lunch?

So, where do animals look for their next meal? Well, a lot of them look at each other! Unless they are plant-eaters, most animals eat other animals. Small animals get eaten by larger ones, which are then eaten by even larger animals. This is called a *food chain*.

To understand where food chains start, you have to look up...all the way up to the sun! Without the sun, there wouldn't be any plants in the ocean. Plants, which come next in food chains, need the sun's energy to grow.

Most of the plants in the ocean are so small, you can only see them with a microscope. These itsy-bitsy floating plants are called *phytoplankton*.

> It might look like the water I'm swimming through is full of a whole lot of nothing, but it's actually filled with life!

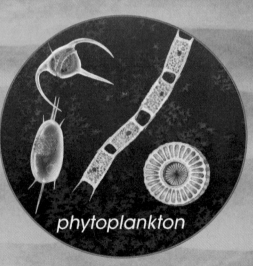

phytoplankton

copepod

Next in most ocean food chains are floating animals called *zooplankton*. These can be the babies of animals such as crabs, shrimp, or fish, or they can be any kind of floating animal that never gets very large, like the copepod.

One ocean food chain might look something like this:

KILLER WHALE     SALMON     HERRING    ZOOPLANKTON   PHYTOPLANKTON

All of these phytoplankton and zooplankton float around in the ocean like peas and carrots in your bowl of soup. Let's find out how some animals slurp this food out of the sea.

## Chains and Webs

Do you only eat peanut butter and jelly sandwiches? Probably not. Ocean animals eat a variety of food, too. So, ocean animals are actually part of a lot of different food chains. Together, all of these food chains are called a food web.

## That's a Mouthful, Mate!

*Phytoplankton* (FIE-toe-plank-tun) and *zooplankton* (ZOO-oh-plank-tun) are big words for some of the most important stuff in the sea! Phytoplankton are floating plants. Zooplankton are floating animals. And usually both are very small.

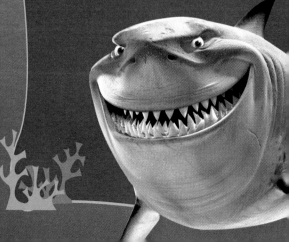

26

# Meet the slurpers

How do animals catch all of that floating food in the ocean? Going after each tiny plankton, one by one, would take way too long! So, animals that eat plankton have ways to strain or filter it out of the water. These animals are called *filter feeders*.

Clams suck in water through tube-like organs called siphons (SYE-funs), and they strain the plankton out of the water using gills.

tube worm

Tube worms gather plankton on a cluster of tentacles that they wave in the water.

Oysters open their shells to let water flow in. They filter out the plankton with their gills.

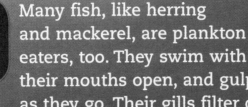
clam with siphon

thorny oyster

Many fish, like herring and mackerel, are plankton eaters, too. They swim with their mouths open, and gulp as they go. Their gills filter out the plankton.

herring

Not all filter feeders are mini-munchers...some can be enormous eaters! Many whales and sharks are filter feeders.

mackerel

Whales, like gray, humpback, or blue whales, trap plankton on long, bristly plates called *baleen*. They take a big gulp of water and then they use their table-sized tongues to push the water back out through the baleen. Then, they slurp up the dinner that's caught on the baleen.

**Baleen of a humpback whale**

# That's a Mouthful, Mate!

*Baleen* (BAY-leen) is made of the same stuff as your fingernails. It's strong but bendable.

What do you think of when you hear the word *shark*? Sharp teeth and lots of them? Not all sharks eat fish or marine mammals. Some sharks, like whale sharks and basking sharks, eat plankton. They catch the plankton on rows of bristles on their gills.

Filter feeding may be fine for many marine animals, but what about those that have a craving for something larger? Let's find out how they chow down.

# Something's Fishy

Ugh! Whale breath stinks. All those little bits of food caught in their baleen and no toothbrush in sight means that you can smell a whale's breath a mile away!

# Meet the CHOMPERS

For many animals, a plate of plankton wouldn't even be a good bedtime snack! Instead, they want something bigger and juicier. It's time to meet the ocean's *predators*! Predators chase, snatch, catch, and eat other animals.

squid

Octopuses and squid quickly swim after their **prey**, which include crabs and fish. Then they kill their prey using their sharp, beak-like mouths before they chomp down.

sea star

A sea star creeps along the ocean bottom until it finds a nice clam or mussel. Then it wraps its arms around the shell and pulls. Once the shell is opened slightly, the sea star squeezes its stomach inside the shell. Strong stomach juices dissolve the sea star's dinner before it eats it up!

## CLOWNING AROUND!

I guess you could say that a sea star always goes *out* for dinner!

Oh, Dad. Just clam it...

## That's a Mouthful, Mate!

A **predator** is an animal that eats other animals. **Prey** is the animal hunted by a predator. So, when a great white shark (other than me, of course) eats a fish, the shark is the predator and the fish is the prey.

harbor seal

common dolphin

sperm whale

Seals, dolphins, most sharks, and whales with teeth (like sperm whales) chase and eat larger prey such as fish or squid. Sharks and killer whales will even eat other sharks or whales. They all use strong, sharp teeth for catching and killing their prey.

Hey, dude, did you know that a sea turtle's favorite food is a nice, juicy jellyfish? We snack on these yummy floating jellies as we swim.

Let's check out the teeth of a great white shark. Great whites have serrated teeth (teeth that look like the edge of a saw) that grow in several rows. Shark teeth fall out all the time. Worn and broken teeth are always being replaced by new ones. Those super-sharp chompers make sharks the most powerful predators in the ocean.

great white shark

Well, it's almost the end of your first day at Undersea School. It's time to start heading home. Did you ever wonder where home is for ocean animals? Let's take a look at a few undersea neighborhoods.

# Chapter 5: Neighborhoods of the Ocean

## A Room at the Reef

Welcome to my neighborhood, the coral reef! Did you know that coral reefs are made of living things? That's right—coral are animals! These tiny animals are smaller than mini-marshmallows, and most of them are protected by a hard skeleton. When the coral die, these hard skeletons are left behind. New coral grow on top of the skeletons, so the reef keeps getting bigger.

Coral grow in all sorts of shapes, like:

brains...

plates...

horns, and...

stars!

### BIRD'S EYE VIEW

**Nigel**
*pelican*

The view of the reef from the sky is great! The largest coral reef in the world, the Great Barrier Reef in Australia, can be seen from space!

# The Great Beyond: The Open Ocean

The edge of the reef (or what we call the "drop-off") is the beginning of the **open ocean**. The open ocean is full of life. The animals that live there swim or float, and they don't need the protection of a reef. You'll find turtles, schools of large tuna, sharks, whales, swordfish, and jellyfish in the open ocean.

school of tuna

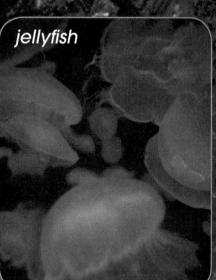
jellyfish

If you're looking for a place to stretch out your fins or take a nice, long swim, then the open ocean is the place for

swordfish

you! But you might not want to swim too deep. The deeper the ocean gets, the less sunlight there is. Without sunlight, plants can't grow, and without plants, there's less food. And when there's less food—it becomes harder to survive.

Are you ready to swim to another neighborhood? Let's check out a place where animals live with their heads in the sand or "glued" to a rock!

**CLOWNING AROUND!**

**Q:** Do you know what's in the middle of the ocean?

**A:** The letter "E"!

32

# Life at the Beach

A sandy beach isn't just a great place to build sand castles. Many creatures actually live in the sand. That sandy home can be on a beach, or in the sand at the bottom of the ocean.

If you're ever walking on a sandy beach, watch out for squirts of water coming out of holes in the sand. Those squirts are coming from clams that live beneath those holes. Don't worry, they're not trying to soak you with mini squirt guns. The water is really coming out of their siphons (a tube used to suck in and spurt out water—see page 27).

*sand dollar*

*moon snail*

Sand dollars are covered with tiny spines, which they use to move along the sand's surface, or to burrow into the sand.

Some snails, like moon snails, live just below the sand's surface. They cruise along searching for prey like clams.

## 🐟 🐟 Something's Fishy 🐟 🐟

*Pssst!* Did you know that sand is filled with lots of tiny creatures that live between the grains of sand? Think of that the next time you take a stroll on a beach!

## CLOWNING AROUND!

**Q:** What sea creatures only come out at night?

**A:** Moon snails and sea stars!

# on the Rocks

If you ever visit a beach you might be able to see one of the coolest homes in the ocean. When the tide is out (and the ocean is farther away from the beach), *rocky shores* are uncovered. Rocky shores are home to all sorts of animals, including sea stars, sea anemones, barnacles, and snails.

tidal pool and sea stars

barnacles

When the tide is out, snails and crabs creep under seaweed or into cracks in the rocks. Barnacles and mussels close up tight to wait for the water to come back in. And fish stay in tidal pools, which are like little swimming pools that are left behind when the tide is low. Animals that live on rocky shores must be able to survive both under the water and above the water.

mussels

Well, that brings us to the end of our undersea neighborhood tour. It's time to dive into some fun with another game. Just keep swimming to the next page!

Just keep swimming, just keep swimming…

# FISHY FUN: Underwater Word Hunt

Put on your hunting goggles! Some of the key words you just learned about have gotten lost among all these letters. Your mission is to hunt for all the words listed in the yellow box below to the left. Words can go down, sideways, or diagonally. Good luck!

*(When you're finished, check your answers on page 38!)*

clam
clown fish
coral reef
dolphin
fish
invertebrate
jellyfish
mammal
plankton
predator
prey
reptile
sea horse
shrimp
turtle
whale

| C | D | A | F | I | S | H | G | W | N | B | D |
|---|---|---|---|---|---|---|---|---|---|---|---|
| R | O | A | A | Y | E | Y | X | S | W | N | O |
| D | D | R | P | L | A | N | K | T | O | N | L |
| P | X | T | A | F | H | O | Z | I | I | D | P |
| R | R | R | C | L | O | W | N | F | I | S | H |
| I | G | Z | Q | U | R | P | U | Q | A | L | I |
| L | H | P | A | Z | S | E | B | E | P | I | N |
| E | K | R | S | I | E | P | E | Y | R | P | P |
| J | E | E | P | H | E | H | C | F | E | Y | Q |
| F | T | Y | M | R | R | L | F | L | D | Y | Z |
| Z | U | Q | A | W | S | I | D | N | A | O | R |
| R | R | G | M | O | X | A | M | P | T | M | W |
| V | T | M | M | U | D | O | B | P | O | L | W |
| H | L | K | A | W | C | B | J | M | R | G | H |
| J | E | L | L | Y | F | I | S | H | J | D | A |
| A | D | Q | L | T | W | P | F | Y | L | B | L |
| I | N | V | E | R | T | E | B | R | A | T | E |

# SHOW·AND·TELL

## with Marine Biologist, Adrienne Mason

I have a new friend I want you to meet! Her name is Adrienne Mason. Adrienne is a marine biologist who loves to teach students, just like us, all about the ocean. I asked Adrienne some questions about her undersea adventures. Here's what she had to say:

**What parts of the ocean have you explored?**

**ADRIENNE:** I'm lucky that I've always lived by the sea. I grew up exploring the beaches near my home on Vancouver Island in Canada. I've traveled a lot and have explored the seashore in India, France, the Caribbean, New Zealand, Tonga, and a few other countries. I've also snorkeled in coral reefs and dove in certain places to about ninety feet.

**What was one of your most exciting undersea adventures?**

**ADRIENNE:** I think it was the first time I ever went scuba diving. I was a bit nervous but very excited, too. About five minutes into the dive I saw these black-and-white birds dart by me. I thought "Penguins!" But I was in the ocean near British Columbia and there are no penguins there. They were actually diving birds called common murres.

common murres

**Have you ever gotten lost in the ocean...kinda like me?**

**ADRIENNE:** No, but I have had to be rescued from the top of the ocean! I was sailing on a ship across the Atlantic and got very sick off the coast of Canada. The Coast Guard had to come and pick me up off the ship and take me to the hospital. I had to have an operation, but everything turned out okay in the end. I was back on the ship after about two weeks of rest.

**Which do you think is the best fish in the ocean...besides me and my dad?**

**ADRIENNE:** Wow, it's tough to decide! There are so many great fish in the sea. One of my favorites is the hagfish. It's not very pretty, but it's really important. Hagfish eat dead things in the sea and they release huge amounts of thick slime to protect themselves. It's a bit gross, but very bizarre and cool, too!

hagfish

**What's the most amazing thing you learned about the ocean?**

**ADRIENNE:** There are so many things. The ocean feeds us, it regulates our climate, it's filled with an incredible variety of living things, it provides us with some medicines...and there's still so much more that hasn't been discovered yet. That's pretty amazing, don't you think?

# School's Out!

Great swimming! We've come to the end of our first journey at Undersea School. You've explored some cool places, made some new friends, and met a few of the creatures that call the ocean home. But Undersea School has just begun. On our future field trips we'll explore all things wet and salty—everything from the deep sea to the marvels of whales and dolphins to ways that humans, like you, travel through the ocean!

"Sea" you next time!

When you finish your classes at Undersea School do you know what you'll get?

Your deep-ploma!

# NEMO'S ANSWER PAGE

**1.** Most of Earth's water is in the O C E A N.
9   6

**2.** The five oceans are named: Pacific, Arctic, Southern, Indian, and
A T L A N T I C.
1   10

**3.** Water can be a solid, gas, or L I Q U I D.
2    3

**4.** The W I N D makes waves in the ocean.
7

**5.** The salt in the ocean comes from soil and R O C K S.
11

**6.** Waves stop at the B E A C H.
5

**7.** E.A.C. stands for East Australian C U R R E N T.
4

**8.** Some fish swim in large groups called, S C H O O L S, for safety.
8

## Fishy Fun:
### A Recess Riddle
*(page 18)*

Did you figure out what game my friends and I like to play at recess?

**T I D E   A N D   S E A-K**
1   2   3   4    5   6   7    8   9   10   11

## Fishy Fun:
### Underwater Word Hunt
*(page 35)*

Did you find all the words? Let's see where they were hiding...

38